We should all be very afraid. He is surely making himself into a tyrant.

Roman orator Cicero, on Caesar, 59 B.C.

〜〜〜〜〜〜〜〜

Julius Caesar rose to become one of the most powerful men in the Roman Republic. When his former allies turned against him, he defeated them in a brutal civil war and declared himself dictator for life. Was Caesar responsible for the downfall of one of history's first great experiments in democracy? Or did he bring order to a system that was already falling apart? Gather the evidence as you read and decide for yourself!

For Paul and Ben, with love.

Photographs ©: akg-images, London: 68 center left, 78 (Vincenzo Pirozzi), 105 (Heinrich Leutemann); Alamy Images: 28 (SuperStock), 32 (Chronicle), 34 (Ivy Close Images), 50, 56, 64, 68 top, 69 center, 99, 118 (Mary Evans Picture Library); Art Resource, NY: 17 (British Library), 21, 136, 137 (Balage Balogh), 31 (Alfredo Dagli Orti/The Art Archive), 37, 69 top (Scala), 52, 66 top (Alinari), 67 center, 75, 109 (Gianni Dagli Orti/The Art Archive); Bridgeman Images: 23 (Ancient Art and Architecture Collection Ltd.), 44, 67 bottom (Peter Newark Historical Pictures), 62 left, 68 center (Louvre, Paris, France), 69 bottom, 97 (Birmingham Museums and Art Gallery), 83 (Archives Charmet), 89, 115 (Look and Learn), 114; Corbis Images: 43 (Stapleton Collection), 58 (Gianni Dagli Orti), 68 bottom (Michael Nicholson), 71 bottom, 117 (Bettmann); DK Images: 70 center; Getty Images: 55 (Bob Thomas/Popperfoto), 62 right, 68 center right (A. Dagli Orti/DEA); Superstock, Inc.: 10 (Stock Montage), 42; The Granger Collection, New York: 27, 47, 66 bottom, 67 top, 70 top, 71 top, 71 center, 98, 101, 111; The Image Works/TopFoto: 70 bottom; Shutterstock: 123, 126, 128 (veronchick84), 132 (BM Design), 22, 23, 101, 122 (Waj)

Illustrations by XNR Productions, Inc.: 4, 5, 8, 9
Cover art, page 8 inset by Mark Summers
Chapter art by Raphael Montoliu

Library of Congress Cataloging-in-Publication Data
Rinaldo, Denise.
Julius Caesar : dictator for life / by Denise Rinaldo. – Revised edition.
pages cm. – (A wicked history)
Includes bibliographical references and index.
ISBN 978-0-531-22123-5 (library binding) – ISBN 978-0-531-22331-4 (pbk.)
1. Caesar, Julius—Juvenile literature. 2. Heads of state—Rome—
Biography—Juvenile literature. 3. Generals—Rome—
Biography—Juvenile literature. 4. Rome—History—Republic,
265-30 B.C.—Juvenile literature. I. Title.
DG261.R56 2015
937'.05092—dc23
[B]

2015019346

Tod Olson, Series Editor
Marie O'Neill, Art Director
Allicette Torres, Cover Design
SimonSays Design!, Book Design and Production

© 2016, 2010 Scholastic Inc.

Julius Caesar

Dictator for Life

DENISE RINALDO

Franklin Watts®
An Imprint of Scholastic Inc.
New York   Toronto   London   Auckland   Sydney
Mexico City   New Delhi   Hong Kong
Danbury, Connecticut

The World of Julius Caesar

Rome dominated the ancient world—and Caesar
was determined to dominate Rome.

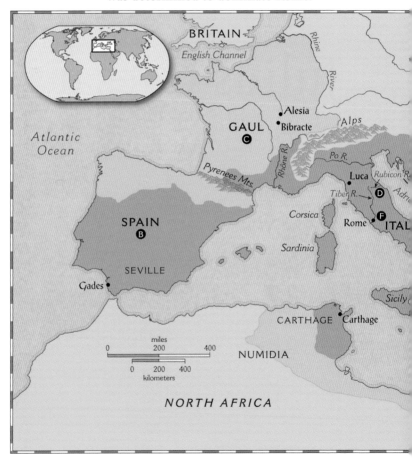

BRITAIN

English Channel

Rhine River

Alesia

GAUL
Bibracte
C

Alps

Atlantic
Ocean

Pyrenees Mts.

Rhône R.

Po R.

Luca

Rubicon R.

Tiber R.

D

Adri

SPAIN
B

Corsica

Rome

F

ITAL

Sardinia

SEVILLE

Gades

Sicily

CARTHAGE Carthage

miles
0   200   400

0   200   400
kilometers

NUMIDIA

NORTH AFRICA

KEY

A In 80 B.C., Caesar started his political career as an aide to the governor of the Province of Asia.

B Caesar served as governor in 62 B.C. before returning to rule Rome as consul.

C Given command of Roman provinces in Gaul in 58 B.C., Caesar spent the next decade bringing Gallic tribes under Roman control.

D In 49 B.C., Caesar crossed the Rubicon River, starting a civil war with his former ally Pompey.

E In 48 B.C., Pompey was killed, and Caesar helped Cleopatra gain the Egyptian throne.

F Caesar was assassinated in 44 B.C. after ruling Rome as dictator for two years.

Roman Republic as of 100 B.C.

Area added by 44 B.C.

Danube River

Black Sea

PARTHIA

MACEDONIA   •Byzantium

undisium

Plain of Pharsalus

iver Enipeus→

GREECE

CORINTH

•Athens

PROVINCE OF ASIA

Aegean Sea   •Mytilene **A**

•Miletus

Euphrates R.

Tigris R.

Rhodes

Crete

Cyprus

N

editerranean Sea

Alexandria •**E**

EGYPT

Nile River

TABLE OF CONTENTS

A Wicked Web

A look at the allies and enemies of Julius Caesar.

Family and Friends

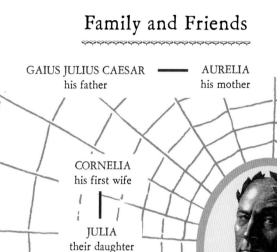

GAIUS JULIUS CAESAR — AURELIA
his father — his mother

CORNELIA
his first wife

JULIA
their daughter

POMPEIA
his second wife

CALPURNIA
his third wife

JULIUS CAESAR

MARIUS
his uncle,
populare leader

CINNA
populare leader and
Caesar's father-in-law

Allies

❦❦❦❦❦❦❦❦❦❦❦❦❦❦❦❦❦❦❦❦❦❦❦

CRASSUS
wealthy politician; member of
the First Triumvirate

POMPEY
member of the First
Triumvirate; later fought a
civil war against Caesar

QUINTUS CASSIUS
tribune who supported
Caesar during the civil war
with Pompey

MARC ANTONY
tribune who supported
Caesar during the civil
war with Pompey

CLEOPATRA
queen of Egypt; may have
had a child with Caesar

Enemies

❦❦❦❦❦❦❦❦❦❦❦❦❦❦❦❦❦❦❦❦❦❦❦

SULLA
optimate leader; forced
young Caesar into exile

SPARTACUS
leader of slave
rebellion against Rome

VERCINGETORIX
leader of Gallic rebellion;
defeated by Caesar

PTOLEMY XIII
pharaoh of Egypt;
defeated by Caesar

CICERO
great orator and
critic of Caesar

CATO
senator who bitterly
opposed Caesar for 20 years

BIBULUS
Caesar's co-consul
and political enemy

MARCUS BRUTUS
member of plot to
assassinate Caesar

JULIUS CAESAR, 100–44 B.C.

IN 75 B.C., JULIUS CAESAR SET OUT FROM Rome on a 1,000-mile journey through the pirate-infested waters of the Mediterranean Sea. He was bound for the Isle of Rhodes, where he hoped to learn the art of oratory from a famous teacher.

It was a long and dangerous trip for a little instruction in public speaking. But in the democratic world of Rome, an aspiring politician needed to be able to stand before a crowd and hold them spellbound with his words. And at 25, Caesar was more than just another aspiring politician. He knew exactly what he wanted out of life: He wanted to rule the greatest city on earth and all its far-flung lands.

Midway through Caesar's journey to Rhodes, his grand plans nearly met an early end. Pirates seized his ship and forced it into port at their island base. The moment the pirates saw Caesar, they knew they'd struck gold. His clothes, his hairstyle, and the way he spoke made it obvious: He was a Roman aristocrat, and his family would probably pay a huge ransom for him.

While the outlaws debated their next move, Caesar showed no fear. He joked with the pirates that he was worth far more than the 20 talents of silver they wanted in return for his freedom. He told them to raise the price to 50. Then he sent his crew to the city of Miletus (in present-day Turkey) to borrow the money.

Caesar spent the next month in the pirate camp writing poems and speeches and reciting them to his captors. When the pirates failed to praise his work heartily enough, he called them "illiterate barbarians." Caesar threatened to return and crucify every one of them after he was set free. The pirates laughed, thinking it was just an idle boast.

They couldn't have been more wrong.

When Caesar's crew returned with the 50 talents, the pirates freed their hostage. Caesar hurried to Miletus. He had no official title and no real authority, yet he talked the city leaders into letting him borrow a small fleet of warships and sailors to man them.

With his instant navy, Caesar sailed back to the pirate base, claimed the pirates' treasure as his own, and took the men prisoner. He brought his captives to a jail near Miletus and ordered the jailers to crucify the men. Although Caesar had no official right to make such an order, the jailers followed his instructions.

Caesar did show the pirates a small amount of mercy. He spared them the agony of a real crucifixion—being nailed alive to a cross. He had each man's throat slashed before he was crucified.

This combination of pride, poise, and ruthlessness would eventually carry Caesar to the height of power. Rome was one of history's first great democracies, and Caesar became its most revered—and most despised—leader. He used Rome's democratic traditions to rise through the ranks. Then he used his power to destroy what had taken decades to build.

*Consider these questions as you read about
Caesar's early life.*

BIG QUESTION:

How was Caesar's character shaped by his family
background and the world in which he lived?

RELATED QUESTIONS:

- How did Caesar's parents view their son? What effect
  do you think their expectations had on how he viewed
  himself?

- How did the young Caesar draw attention to himself?

- Why did Caesar marry Cinna's daughter Cornelia?
  What did this help him achieve?

- Describe some actions taken by the young Caesar that
  demonstrate courage.

Young

Caesar

C H A P T E R 1

At the Center
of the World

Caesar is born into a noble family
WITH GREAT AMBITIONS.

I̵T WAS A SUMMER DAY IN ROME IN THE
year 100 B.C. In a modest home on the outskirts of a
wealthy neighborhood, Aurelia, the wife of Gaius Julius
Caesar, gave birth to a baby boy.

Aurelia and Gaius made sure that their son was
healthy and likely to survive. Then they did what they
could to ensure his success in life. They named him
after his father so it would be clear from his family

JULIUS CAESAR was born into one of Rome's oldest families.
But contrary to this depiction, the Caesars had fallen on hard times.
Unlike the rich families of Rome, they lived in an apartment
building in a crowded neighborhood.

names, Julius and Caesar, that he came from noble birth.
In keeping with Roman tradition, they probably lit fires
of thanksgiving on stone altars in their home. They
made sacrifices to the gods. On the tenth day of their
new child's life, they would have watched for patterns
formed by birds in flight, hoping for a sign that great
things were in store for Julius.

Caesar's parents raised their son to believe he had a
special destiny.

His father's family members weren't wealthy, and they hadn't held positions of great power in many generations. But they were patricians, nobles who traced their history back to the very beginning of Rome. They claimed to be descended from Venus, the Roman goddess of love and beauty. And Caesar's aunt Julia had married well. Her husband, Marius, had recently won fame as a war hero for battling rebellious Germanic tribes in the northern provinces.

Aurelia's family had a less illustrious history but more success in the recent past. Her father, grandfather, and three of her cousins had served as *consul*, Rome's highest political office.

Parents such as these expected their son to bring glory to the family, and they made sure his education prepared him for the task. Caesar probably learned basic math and reading from his mother. After that, a tutor took over—a former slave named Marcus Antonius Gnipho, who was known as an excellent teacher of Greek and Latin.

Under Gnipho's instruction, Caesar learned to read, write, and debate in both Latin and Greek. He studied the history of Rome through epic stories about gods, heroes, and great battles. Captivated by the tales, he learned to take great pride in his homeland.

Rome, after all, was the center of the world to nearly everyone who knew of its existence. In the 50 years before Caesar's birth, Roman armies had destroyed Carthage, the North African trading empire that had dominated the Mediterranean for centuries. They had taken over the great kingdom of Macedonia, north of Greece. By 100 B.C., Rome dominated almost all the land around the Mediterranean Sea. Even the great Egyptian pharaohs paid tribute to the rulers of Rome.

Yet for all their military might, the Romans took at least as much pride in their political institutions. Rome was a republic—a government in which people elect their own leaders. It had been formed 400 years earlier, when the Roman people overthrew a tyrannical king. They had jealously guarded their freedoms ever since.

When Caesar passed the age of seven, he got to explore the bustling city of Rome firsthand. He probably started accompanying his father to the Senate, where Gaius held political office. Father and son would have made their way through crowded streets that pulsed with activity. Horse-drawn chariots sped through the narrow lanes on their way to races in the city center. Slaves seized by victorious Roman armies carried their masters aloft on litters. Pedestrians from all walks of life made their way to Rome's food markets, raucous taverns, and vast public baths.

Caesar and his father arrived each morning at the Forum, the open square that housed the Senate. There, merchants sold fashionable goods, and worshippers gathered at lavish marble temples. Legislators debated issues and made laws, judges held trials, politicians gave speeches. All business in the Forum, no matter how controversial, was open to the public.

THE FORUM stood at the center of Rome. Citizens came there to worship in marble temples, to argue politics, and to cheer victorious armies on their return from foreign lands.

This was Caesar's Rome. It stood as the biggest, most powerful city in the world, home to hundreds of thousands of people. Its citizens enjoyed political freedoms unknown anywhere else on earth. And yet, as Caesar began to plan his future, the world around him trembled with violence. A civil war was about to break out that would bring terror to Rome and change Caesar's life forever.

Who Ruled Rome?

IN CAESAR'S TIME, RICH ARISTOCRATS HELD THE most powerful positions in government, but all Roman citizens, no matter how poor, made their voices heard.

Citizens were Romans with special rights, including the right to vote and the right not to pay taxes. (Most of Rome's wealth came from conquered provinces, whose people were not citizens.) Women and slaves, in addition to residents of the provinces, were excluded from citizenship.

Tribunes of the People were officials elected by the common people of Rome to protect their rights. They had the right to veto laws and official acts, and they often came into conflict with Rome's top officials—the magistrates.

The Popular Assembly was a legislative body made up of Roman citizens. All citizens who were not senators voted in the Assembly. They had the power to approve the Senate's choice of magistrates, declare war, decide judicial cases, and pass legislation.

THE SENATE
was Rome's most
powerful political
body. It was
founded more than
600 years
before Julius
Caesar's birth.

The Senate was made up of about 300 of Rome's richest and most powerful men. Senators advised the magistrates, prepared legislation, and handled relations with foreign governments. They were not elected, but appointed based on their wealth, family background, and political experience.

Magistrates were the top government officials. These men usually came from the ranks of the aristocracy. They held the offices of censor, consul, praetor, aedile, and quaestor.

CHAPTER 2

Civil War!

The streets of Rome turn into a battleground, and CAESAR IS CAUGHT IN THE MIDDLE.

WHEN CAESAR WAS 12, ROME BEGAN TO slide toward a bloody civil war, and Caesar's uncle Marius was at the center of the chaos.

Marius, who was not of noble birth, had risen to power with the help of Rome's poorer classes. He won the consulship in 107 B.C. by telling voters that his skill as a soldier made him more qualified than his wealthy rivals. Most aristocrats, he claimed, had little to offer besides a famous family name.

When Marius asked for troops to fight a war in North Africa, his opponents in the Senate refused to give him an army of professional soldiers. So Marius raised an army himself. His soldiers were poor farmers and laborers who volunteered in return for a share of any treasure they might plunder in battle. Marius and his army of commoners went on to conquer the Kingdom of Numidia in North Africa and subdue the Germanic tribes to the north.

In 91 B.C., Marius met his match. A revolt broke out in the nearby Italian provinces, and the rebels fought Marius to a standstill. Convinced that Marius was no longer the strong leader he had once been, the Senate sent a general named Sulla to finish the job. Sulla successfully put down the rebellion and returned to Rome a hero.

In 88 B.C., as a reward for his exploits, Sulla was elected consul. The Senate then gave him command of an army to put down a rebellion in the Province of Asia (in present-day Turkey).

Marius was enraged by Sulla's success. He wanted the command for himself and made a risky move to get it. He met with a *tribune*, a leader of the Popular Assembly, and proposed a trade. He would work to give the Assembly more power. In return, the Assembly would overrule the Senate, strip Sulla of his command, and give it to Marius.

The Assembly did exactly as Marius asked—and Rome suffered the consequences. When Sulla heard the news, he gathered his army and marched it to the gates of Rome. The sight threw the city into a panic; never before had Roman soldiers marched on their own city.

After brushing aside envoys from Marius, Sulla stood by while his men marched through the gates of the city. They fought off a small force loyal to Marius and then stormed through the streets, burning down houses and terrorizing innocent Romans. At Sulla's command, the tribune who had convinced the Assembly to support Marius was killed. Marius fled, and many of the allies he left behind were murdered.

IN 88 B.C., Sulla led his army into Rome and slaughtered Marius's allies. As the Romans gobbled up more territory, the generals they sent to fight in distant lands grew harder to control.

Sulla stayed in Rome long enough to ensure that his allies were firmly in control. Then he took his army and went east to fight his war in Asia.

The war at home, however, was just beginning. For the first time, Rome seemed to be splitting into factions. Sulla represented the *optimates*, or "best men," who wanted to protect the interests of Rome's noble families by extending the power of the Senate. Marius represented the *populares*, who used the Popular

CAESAR'S UNCLE MARIUS (right) begs for death. He had fled
Rome after his rival, Sulla, stormed the city and murdered
his allies. Marius feared that it was only a matter of time before
Sulla had him killed as well.

Assembly to get their way and claimed to be looking
out for the poor citizens of Rome.

In 87 B.C., the populares took advantage of Sulla's
absence. Marius returned with a thuggish band of freed
slaves acting as his personal bodyguards. He joined up
with a general named Cinna, and together they stormed
into Rome. They quickly overwhelmed Sulla's allies and
had dozens of them executed. The victors had the heads

of their rivals nailed to the speaker's platform in the Forum for all to see.

As Marius and Cinna took control of Rome, Caesar was nearing the age of 14. According to Roman custom, he was nearly an adult. He probably cut his boyish locks into the close-cropped hairstyle befitting a man. He put aside the purple-trimmed toga reserved for boys and *magistrates* and put on the plain white of an adult citizen.

It could not have been an easy time to take on the responsibilities of an adult. Twice in two years, rival armies had turned the streets of Rome into a battleground. Then in 86 B.C., Caesar's uncle Marius died, leaving the Republic in control of the ruthless Cinna. Life in the city Caesar loved seemed to be spinning out of control.

Then, just before Caesar turned 16, personal tragedy struck. His father died suddenly, collapsing on the doorstep. Now Caesar took over as the head of his family, left to fend for himself in a troubled city.

CHAPTER 3

Blood in
the Streets

Caesar's life is put in danger when
HIS ALLY CINNA IS MURDERED.

WITHOUT A FATHER TO GUIDE HIM,
Caesar planned his future on his own. He desperately
wanted to be part of Rome's ruling elite, but so did
hundreds of other ambitious young noblemen.

Even as a teenager, Caesar found ways to make himself
stand out from the crowd. His dark, wavy hair was always
perfectly cut and combed. He wore his toga with a jauntily
tied belt while most of his friends let theirs hang loose.

JULIUS CAESAR'S teenage years were marked by the deaths of his father and his uncle—the tyrant Marius. But Caesar managed to protect himself by marrying the daughter of Cinna, Rome's current strongman.

Like most upper-class boys, he learned horsemanship. But Caesar made sure to be seen riding bareback, his arms folded behind him, steering the horse with his knees.

For all Caesar's showmanship, he lacked two more important assets: money and powerful friends. He needed a wealthy ally, and the best way to get one was through marriage. So, at age 16, Caesar got himself noticed by Cinna, the most powerful man in Rome. Cinna had a 13-year-old daughter named Cornelia, and in 84 B.C., he offered her hand in marriage to Caesar. Cinna must have thought the cocky young man would one day make a powerful son-in-law.

Cinna, however, barely lived long enough to witness the wedding. He heard that Marius's old rival, Sulla, was marching back to Rome. Cinna immediately declared Sulla an enemy of the state and led an army out to destroy him. They hadn't gotten far when Cinna's men decided they didn't stand a chance against Sulla. They mutinied and murdered Cinna miles from home.

CAESAR LOST HIS LAST ALLY when his father-in-law, Cinna, was murdered by his own troops. After Cinna's death, Sulla returned to Rome and terrorized anyone who had backed this populare leader.

With Rome's most powerful leader out of the way, Sulla came storming back. One fall day in 82 B.C., cries of "*Sulla ad portas!*"—"Sulla is at the gates!"—rang out through the city. Sulla led his men into Rome, and for the third time in six years, the streets were filled with the sound of clashing swords.

Sulla triumphed quickly and vowed revenge against his populare enemies. With his army in control of the city, he forced the Senate to name him *dictator*— sole ruler of Rome. Then he began posting lists of his enemies in the Forum. People on the lists were stripped of their legal rights and could be killed for a reward. Their families' property was confiscated and distributed among Sulla's allies. Soon the bodies of the dictator's enemies could be seen floating in the Tiber River. Severed heads were displayed on stakes in the Forum.

Caesar must have worried that this reign of terror would claim him as well. He was married to the daughter of Sulla's archenemy. Surely it was only a

AFTER RETURNING TO ROME, Sulla posted lists of his
many enemies. Everyone on the lists was to be killed on sight.
Screams from the executed could even be heard while Sulla
calmly gave speeches at the Forum.

matter of time before his name appeared on one of the
lists. If it did, he would face a grisly death at the hands
of Sulla's henchmen.

Despite the dangers, Caesar fought the instinct to
flee. He decided to stick it out in Rome and wait for his
fate to unfold.

Making a Stand

Caesar is offered a choice:
HIS MARRIAGE OR HIS LIFE.

MONTHS PASSED, MARKED BY EXECUTION after execution, but Caesar's name did not appear on any of Sulla's lists. Caesar may have been too poor or insignificant to make his death worth the effort. Or perhaps Sulla, like Cinna before him, thought Caesar might someday make an extremely powerful ally.

Whatever the case, Sulla finally summoned Caesar to a meeting in 81 B.C. Caesar made his way across Rome to talk to the dictator, knowing that his future depended on the outcome of the conversation.

Sulla opened the meeting by mocking Caesar's fussy toga and fancy hairdo. Then he got down to business. Sulla demanded that Caesar cut his ties to Cinna's family by divorcing Cinna's daughter. Staring down the man who ruled Rome with an iron fist, Caesar refused to end his marriage.

For a young and relatively powerless noble, it was a bold—maybe suicidal—decision. During his months as dictator, Sulla had been ruthless in extending his own power. He had passed laws that increased the influence of the Senate and left the tribunes of the people almost powerless. He had ordered the deaths of some 9,000 enemies.

For months, Sulla tried to force Caesar into submission. Finally, the dictator gave up and ordered the stubborn young man arrested. Fearing for his life, Caesar had no choice but to flee.

Still just 19 years old, Caesar became a fugitive in the hills and caves of central Italy. He may have brought slaves or friends to help him, but life on the run

THE DICTATOR SULLA was the most feared man in Rome. Caesar's uncle and father-in-law had been two of Sulla's fiercest enemies. But the optimate leader chose to spare Caesar.

could not have been easy. Sulla's men prowled the countryside looking for enemies of the state, and Caesar had to move every night to stay one step ahead of them.

Luckily for Caesar, his mother had important relatives who had sided with Sulla during the civil wars. They pleaded with the dictator to have mercy on Caesar. For reasons that no one completely understood, Sulla relented. He called off the hunt and pardoned Caesar. At the same time, he made a prediction: "In this young man there is more than one Marius. He will one day deal the death blow to the optimate cause."

Consider these questions as you read about Caesar's rise to power.

BIG QUESTION:

How did Caesar prepare himself for the highest political office in Rome?

RELATED QUESTIONS:

- What did Caesar do at his Aunt Julia's funeral that shows his political savvy? Do you think his actions were genuine, self-serving—or both?

- Caesar identified strongly with Alexander the Great; what does this reveal about his self-image?

- Describe some of Caesar's achievements as consul. What do they tell you about his ability to lead?

🏛

PART 2

Path to Power

CHAPTER 5

Education of a Leader

Caesar lays the groundwork for a
LONG RISE TO THE TOP.

Now 20 YEARS OLD, CAESAR HAD SURVIVED
the most violent years in the recent history of Rome.
He had defied a vengeful dictator and lived to tell the
tale. He had displayed courage, self-assurance, and an
unyielding will.

Yet none of those qualities would get him elected
to one of Rome's high offices. He had no experience
in the day-to-day details of public service, he had not

distinguished himself in battle, and he had never stood in the Forum to dazzle an audience with his eloquence.

Those shortcomings would have to be resolved—and Caesar spent the next decade doing just that.

In 80 B.C., Caesar journeyed 1,000 miles east to the Province of Asia, on the eastern shore of the Aegean Sea. Service in the provinces was a rite of passage that most young nobles undertook at one time or another. They worked for the governor of one of Rome's outlying territories, hoping to win military glory and the kind of political experience that would get them a Senate appointment when they returned home.

Provinces were vitally important to Rome. They produced taxes to fund the military and the government. They supplied the slaves that kept homes, government, and farms running. Often, they served as buffers between Rome and its unconquered enemies. And the governorship of a province was a prize post that could make its recipient wildly rich from bribes and plundered treasure.

The governor of the Province of Asia put Caesar's charm and speaking skills to good use on several diplomatic missions. Then he sent Caesar to war in the Aegean Sea, against the rebellious island city of Mytilene.

No record survives of Caesar's exploits during the campaign, but he must have fought bravely. He won Rome's second-highest award for courage in war, the Civic Crown. For the rest of his life, he proudly wore the crown at official events. (It was rumored that he did so because the headpiece conveniently covered his bald spot.)

In 78 B.C., word reached the Province of Asia that Sulla had died. Caesar returned to Rome, where he found

JULIUS CAESAR wearing his Civic Crown. This wreath was only awarded to Romans who saved fellow citizens by killing at least one enemy and driving the rest from the battlefield.

optimate and populare politicians grappling for control of the Republic. He was approached by one of the leading populares, but wisely decided to stay independent. Instead, he became a lawyer.

Caesar spent the next three years arguing legal cases in the Forum. In ancient Rome, any citizen had the right to bring legal charges against another, and the trials were held in public. Like many young politicians, Caesar used the courts as a way to get attention and build a following.

A POLITICIAN ADDRESSES AN AUDIENCE AT THE FORUM. Caesar was a natural at public events like this. He pressed for the rights of the common Roman citizens, and they began to view him as their champion.

Apparently, he did his job with little concern for its dangers. He earned himself some powerful enemies by trying to prosecute important politicians for corruption.

In 75 B.C., Caesar decided it would be wise to get out of Rome for a while. He set off for Rhodes to sharpen

IN 75 B.C., CAESAR WAS KIDNAPPED by pirates. Rather than showing any fear, he mocked their taste in poetry and scolded them when they disturbed his sleep. After they released him, Caesar returned with soldiers to cut their throats and crucify their corpses.

his public speaking skills. It was on this trip that he crucified the pirates who were unlucky enough to choose him as a hostage.

Caesar returned to Rome in 73 B.C., filled with ambition and confidence. He continued his prosecutions in the Forum, and his reputation as an orator grew. So did his standing as a man about town. He became a fixture at the lavish banquets and dinner parties held by the city's aristocracy. Along with other noble guests, he reclined on couches and savored exotic treats such as snails and sow's womb. He spent his nights charming men and women alike with his fashionable appearance and witty conversation.

Around 72 B.C., Caesar ran for his first political office, as a military tribune—an officer who shared command of a 5,000-man army called a legion. It couldn't have surprised many Romans when he won the election.

CHAPTER 6

Going Public

For the first time, Caesar hears his name CHANTED IN THE STREETS.

CAESAR BEGAN HIS TERM AS A MILITARY tribune just as Rome was battling its way through yet another bloody rebellion. This time, the challenge came from the hundreds of thousands of slaves who cleaned the homes of Rome's aristocracy, built their temples, and fought to the death in their stadiums.

In 73 B.C., a slave named Spartacus led 70,000 of his fellow captives in an uprising against their masters. For two years the rebels fought the mighty Roman armies to a draw. Finally, the uprising came to a brutal end with the crucifixion of 6,000 slaves along the main road leading out of Rome.

It's not clear whether Caesar played a part in defeating Spartacus. But two men who became heroes during the rebellion would later play important roles in Caesar's life. Crassus, a wealthy businessman and ruthless general, won the final battle against Spartacus's

SPARTACUS collapses as the last of his army is destroyed by the legions of Crassus. Spartacus had escaped from gladiator school and raised an army of about 70,000 slaves.

army and ordered the mass crucifixions. Pompey, a dashing and popular commander with his own private army, arrived late on the scene but took credit for aiding in the victory.

After the uprising, Crassus and Pompey were elected consuls and immediately began to roll back the laws that Sulla had passed to curb the power of the populares. Caesar supported the two consuls and took some of the credit when power was restored to the tribunes of the people.

By 70 B.C., Caesar had a budding reputation as a champion of the common man. He turned 30 that year, old enough to run for office as a *quaestor*, the lowest-ranking magistrate in Rome's political hierarchy. Like other candidates for public office, he made himself visible in the Forum in a bright white toga. He greeted members of the Popular Assembly and vowed to defend the interests of Rome's poor.

His efforts paid off, winning him a quaestorship and a place in the Senate. As quaestor, he would be sent to the province of Spain, where he would take care of financial matters for its governor. But as Caesar prepared to leave, his wife, Cornelia, died suddenly at the age of 27. The couple had enjoyed a happy marriage for 14 years. Caesar made sure she had a grand public funeral, even though such an event wasn't common for a young woman.

He also held another public funeral before he left, this one for his aunt Julia. Julia had been married to Sulla's old rival Marius, who was so despised by optimate leaders that for years it had been illegal to utter his name or display his image in Rome.

On the day of Julia's funeral, Caesar took a bold step. He walked to the speaker's platform in the Forum, followed by a procession of slaves carrying huge portraits of Marius. The sight outraged optimate senators, but it thrilled the common people, who had worshiped Marius as one of their own.

Caesar spoke to the crowd about his fierce pride in his family history. He took the opportunity to remind them of his descent from Roman kings and the goddess Venus. The response was startling. Crowds streamed through the streets chanting Marius's name. But the chants of "Julius Caesar!" were nearly as loud.

With the cries of the crowd still echoing in his mind,

CAESAR STARES IN ENVY at a statue honoring Alexander the Great. Alexander had conquered the known world after 12 years of constant war. To match Alexander, Caesar would need to seize control of Rome and all its territories.

Caesar left for Spain. He spent his days overseeing the accounts of the province and settling disputes among its people. The work, however, left him daydreaming of greater achievements. One afternoon, his travels brought him to the ancient city of Gades (present-day Cadiz). He went to pay his respects at a temple there and saw a statue of the heroic Macedonian general Alexander the Great.

Alexander had conquered land from Greece to India by the time he died at the age of 32. According to the ancient historian Suetonius, Caesar realized that he had "done nothing noteworthy at a time of life when Alexander had already brought the world to his feet."

Filled with a sense of urgency, Caesar asked to be released from his post in Spain. He returned to Rome to make his mark on the world.

ROME'S POLITICAL LADDER

CONSUL WAS THE TOP POLITICAL JOB IN ROME. To get there, a man had to climb the ladder of Rome's government, step by step. None of the offices paid a salary; citizens had to be independently wealthy to hold one.

CONSUL: two men elected to one-year terms
DUTIES: Serve as co-heads of Rome's government; command the Republic's armies.
CAESAR'S FIRST TERM: 59 B.C.

PRAETOR: eight men elected to one-year terms
DUTIES: Judge in trials; govern or fight in a consul's absence. After a year in office, a praetor is sent to rule a province.
CAESAR ELECTED: 62 B.C.

AEDILE: four men elected to one-year terms
DUTIES: Take care of Rome's streets and public buildings; put on games and shows to entertain the people.
CAESAR ELECTED: 65 B.C.

CAESAR climbs the ladder.

QUAESTOR: 20 men elected to one-year terms
DUTIES: Manage the finances of Rome or one of its provinces.
CAESAR ELECTED: c. 69 B.C.; he served in Spain.

CHAPTER 7

Let the Games Begin

Caesar entertains Rome with
ARMORED GLADIATORS
AND WILD BEASTS.

BACK IN ROME BY 67 B.C., CAESAR PREPARED
to take his next step up the ladder of political success.
He married Pompeia, a granddaughter of Sulla. In
addition, he sought the attention of Pompey and
Crassus, two of the most powerful men in the Republic.

Pompey was lobbying for control of a huge army
created to fight pirates in the Mediterranean Sea. But

many senators were uneasy with the idea of giving Rome's most popular general such a powerful position. Caesar spoke passionately in Pompey's favor, and Pompey won the command.

Caesar also reached out to Crassus, who became the latest in a series of powerful men to see promise in the young politician. Crassus began to offer loans to fund Caesar's political ambitions, and Caesar put the money to good use.

In 65 B.C., with the help of a few well-placed bribes, Caesar won election to the office of *aedile*. The new position put him in charge of games and entertainment in Rome. It was a perfect way to win the attention of the city's pleasure-seeking masses. Caesar attacked his new job with a flair for the dramatic. He staged free chariot races that drew more than a hundred thousand spectators to a stadium known as the Circus Maximus. He imported wild animals from Africa and had them do battle with slaves and with each other.

Most popular of all was the barbaric Roman tradition

A CHARIOT RACE before a packed audience. As aedile, it was Caesar's job to entertain the common citizens by staging chariot races, gladiator fights, and other games.

of the gladiator show. Gladiators were slaves who were forced to fight each other before a cheering audience. On horseback or on foot, they battled—often to the death—with daggers, tridents, and spears.

Caesar's gladiator shows were the most brutal and elaborate Rome had ever seen. For one such spectacle, staged to honor his father's memory, Caesar brought 320

IN THIS 1872 PAINTING, a victorious gladiator stands over an opponent, who begs the audience to spare his life. The crowd responds by giving the thumbs-down, condemning the fallen gladiator to death. Historians disagree about whether ancient Romans actually used the thumbs-down gesture to signal that a gladiator should be killed.

pairs of armor-clad gladiators into the city. The sheer number of fighting men led some senators to suspect that Caesar was planning to overthrow the government.

Caesar also used his post to remind people of his connection with Marius, who remained a folk hero among the poor. Caesar had artists create portraits and sculptures of his uncle. In the dark of night, he took them to a hill overlooking the Forum. As day broke, citizens stood in the Forum marveling at the display and taking note of Caesar's nerve.

The secret art show attracted the attention of senators as well, many of whom were beginning to fear Caesar's ambition. The Senate called a meeting to discuss the actions of their brash young colleague. "This Caesar is no longer trying to undermine the Republic secretly," complained one optimate senator, "but is now attacking the state openly."

Whatever his standing in the Senate, Caesar was fast becoming a celebrity. He escaped punishment for his prank at the Forum and continued his work as Rome's entertainment director. But staging bloody shows for hundreds of thousands of people proved to be an expensive job. He had to pay for his public spectacles with private money and took out massive loans to cover the expenses. He had also developed a taste for the finer things in life. He collected paintings and pearls. He built a luxurious country house—then had it torn down because he decided he didn't like it.

THIS 2,000-YEAR-OLD ARTWORK shows lions and gladiators battling in a Roman arena. Most gladiators were slaves, but some were Roman citizens who had volunteered in the hopes of winning money or glory.

Caesar was accumulating enormous debt, and it put a lot of pressure on his political career. People like Crassus hadn't lent money out of friendship—they expected Caesar to reach high office and repay them with political favors. Success had become more than an obsession for Caesar; it was a necessity.

Ruler of Rome

Caesar takes control at last—
FOR BETTER OR WORSE.

CAESAR DID NOT DISAPPOINT THE
creditors who had invested in his political success. Over
the next five years he continued his climb through the
ranks. He appeared in court to prosecute senators for
unfairly profiting from their posts in the provinces.
In the Senate, he championed a law to distribute state
land to Rome's poor. In 62 B.C., he was elected a *praetor*,
the final stepping stone toward a consulship.

Caesar also paid huge bribes to be elected Rome's
high priest. That put him in charge of public rituals

and the building of temples. The high priesthood carried with it great prestige, not to mention an enormous official residence at the eastern end of the Forum.

After enjoying his new home in the heart of Rome for little more than a year, Caesar once again went abroad. All praetors were given command of a province after their year in office, and Caesar became governor of Spain. There, he led Roman armies against rebellious tribes, bringing order to a region that had troubled Rome for decades. He plundered enough wealth to make a dent in his debts. Then he returned to Rome, certain that he was ready to occupy the highest office in the Republic.

Caesar entered the city as the favorite to win a consulship. But Rome was now paralyzed by squabbling politicians. A small group of optimates dominated the Senate, blocking any laws put forward by men who might challenge their power. Caesar needed a way to break the resistance of the optimates—and he found it in an alliance with two old and powerful friends, Pompey and Crassus.

As the election for consul approached, Caesar brought Pompey and Crassus together. The two men had been rivals for years, but they now shared a common enemy—the Senate. Crassus had recently had his business interests opposed by jealous senators. Those same senators were trying to deny Pompey the state land he needed to give as payment to his soldiers.

Pompey and Crassus put aside their differences and agreed to work with Caesar. According to the historian Suetonius, they resolved "that no step should be taken in public affairs which did not suit any one of the three." To seal the deal, Caesar arranged for his 16-year-old daughter, Julia, to marry Pompey, who was 47 at the time.

The alliance between the three men became known as "The First Triumvirate." And with Pompey's military might, Crassus's money, and Caesar's popularity, the triumvirate stood ready to dominate Rome.

CRASSUS AND POMPEY (left and right) had once been rivals, but Caesar convinced them to join him in a three-man alliance. With Crassus's wealth, Pompey's military fame, and Caesar's charisma, they were a powerful triumvirate.

In 59 B.C., Caesar and an optimate named Bibulus were elected consuls. Caesar immediately began to impose his will on the Senate. He pressed for broad reforms, including a bill to distribute land to Pompey's veterans and the urban poor.

The land reform bill was the most important of Caesar's laws, and he was ruthless in getting it passed. All consuls had a force of special bodyguards known as *lictors*, and Caesar didn't hesitate to put them to work. When a senator named Cato tried to stop the Senate from voting on the bill, Caesar had his lictors drag the tribune from the Forum and throw him in jail for three days.

When the Senate still refused to act, Caesar took the bill directly to the Popular Assembly. On the day scheduled for the vote, a crowd gathered in the Forum. The triumvirate had stationed armed veterans from Pompey's army at strategic locations around the meeting place.

Caesar spoke first, in favor of the bill. Then Bibulus rose to speak against it. As co-consul, Bibulus had the power to cancel the meeting and keep the Assembly from voting. But he never got the chance. Instead he found himself besieged by Pompey's armed henchmen, who dumped manure on his head. Humiliated and fearing for his life, Bibulus spent the rest of his term confined to his home. He spent his time writing attacks on Caesar's brazen abuse of power and smuggling them out to be posted in the Forum.

A CROWD CHEERS as the optimate Bibulus speaks out against Caesar. Bibulus and Caesar were co-consuls, but with the backing of thugs, Caesar overrode Bibulus.

In the late fall of 59 B.C., Caesar's one-year term as consul neared its end. In that short time, he had solved problems that had plagued Rome for decades. He eased terrible crowding by giving land outside the city to the poor. He cut burdensome taxes. Pompey's loyal soldiers were given farms in return for their years of service.

Caesar also pushed through legislation that made it harder for corrupt Roman governors to make excessive profits from their provinces. Even the famous orator Cicero, one of Caesar's toughest critics, called the anti-corruption law "most just and best."

But Caesar had always been more interested in power than justice. With his consulship about to expire, he needed another outlet for his ambition. He wanted riches to rival Crassus's fortune, military glory to rival Pompey's reputation, and an army loyal to him alone. To achieve his goals he needed an important province to call his own. Before he left office at the end of the year, Caesar got the Senate to grant him a five-year term as commander in Gaul, a vast territory on Rome's northern border.

Part of Gaul had been settled into provinces, where Caesar would have the right to collect taxes. The rest was a land of unconquered tribes, where treasure and military glory were ripe for the picking.

Julius Caesar in Pictures

YOUNG PATRICIAN

Caesar was born in Rome, the city
that ruled almost the entire known
world. He came from a noble family,
which meant that he was eligible for
election to Rome's highest offices.

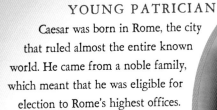

WHERE THE ACTION WAS

The Forum was the political and spiritual heart of Rome. As a child,
Caesar came here to learn from the era's most talented orators.

BLOOD IN THE STREETS

In 88 B.C., General Sulla sent an army to kill his rivals in Rome. This was the first time a Roman army had attacked its own capital—but it wouldn't be the last.

BUDDING HERO

Caesar got his first taste of war in 80 B.C. when he was sent to subdue a rebellious Greek city. He won a Civic Crown (right) for saving the life of a fellow Roman citizen.

KIDNAPPED!

Caesar showed his courage—and his cruelty—when he was kidnapped by pirates in 75 B.C. He joked with his captors and then had them executed after he was freed.

BLOOD SPORTS

As aedile, Caesar threw himself into the job of entertaining the Roman masses. He went into debt to bring hundreds of gladiators to Rome.

TRIPLE THREAT

In 60 B.C., Caesar, Crassus, and Pompey (from left to right) formed an unstoppable alliance. Caesar had the love of Rome's commoners, Pompey was a military hero, and Crassus was rich.

ON THE WARPATH

Caesar's army used siege towers like this one to break into Gallic towns that resisted Roman rule.

DEAR DIARY...

Caesar writing his *Commentaries*. In this journal, he praised his own brilliance in battle.

CROSSING THE RUBICON

After his victories in Gaul, Caesar defied Pompey by leading his army across the Rubicon River and into the Roman heartland. The act was basically a declaration of war.

DECAPITATED

Pompey's head is presented to Caesar, who turns away in dismay. The Egyptian pharaoh, Ptolemy XIII, had killed Pompey in an attempt to win favor with Caesar.

QUEEN CLEOPATRA VII

In 48 B.C., Cleopatra smuggled herself into Caesar's headquarters to ask him to help her take the throne of Egypt from her brother Ptolemy.

FAKE LAKE

In 46 B.C., Caesar built a lake to re-enact a famous naval battle. In A.D. 80, Emperor Titus continued the tradition by staging a mock battle in the flooded Colosseum (right).

DOWN TO BUSINESS

After winning the civil war that had ravaged the Roman Republic, Caesar launched many projects to boost the economy, such as building this magnificent market on the site of the old Forum.

FOR ME?

Caesar rejects a crown offered by his ally Mark Antony. Caesar had been named "dictator for life," but he wanted Romans to think that he had no desire to become king.

RINGLEADERS

Marcus Brutus (left) and Gaius Cassius (right) were two of the major conspirators in the plot to assassinate Caesar.

DEATH OF CAESAR

Slaves carrying the corpse of Julius Caesar. The dictator was dead, but so was Roman democracy. Caesar's nephew, Octavian, would become an emperor with unlimited power.

Consider these questions as you read about Caesar's triumphant rise and brutal fall as dictator of Rome.

BIG QUESTION:

What led to Caesar's downfall?

RELATED QUESTIONS:

- How did Caesar's time in Gaul strengthen his power and reputation? Are his *Commentaries* propaganda?
- What factors led Caesar to start a civil war?
- Describe some positive and negative aspects of Caesar's rule.

🏛

PART 3

War and Dictatorship

CHAPTER 9

First Blood

Caesar and his legions
WREAK HAVOC IN GAUL.

IN THE SPRING OF 58 B.C., CAESAR HAND-picked a group of senior army officers, left the squabbling senators of Rome behind, and hurried northwest toward Gaul.

There he would find a land big enough to satisfy his ambitions. Gaul encompassed all of present-day France and Belgium, as well as parts of Holland, Germany, Switzerland, and northern Italy. Spread across the territory were about 200 Gallic tribes, many of them independent—and determined to stay that way.

The southeastern part of Gaul had already been conquered by Rome; Caesar vowed to subdue the rest. The army charged with the job consisted of four legions—fighting units of 5,000 well-trained professional soldiers. The legions were scattered across southeastern Gaul, and Caesar took command of one on his way north.

Caesar's men cut an impressive sight as they labored across the 15,000-foot peaks of the Alps. The legionnaires wore chain-mail armor and bronze helmets. They each carried a six-foot javelin with an iron point heavy enough to pierce an opponent's shield. Two-foot swords with sharp steel blades hung from their waists, ready for hand-to-hand combat.

As soon as he cleared the

A ROMAN SOLDIER with his sword, shield, and javelin. Romans fought shoulder-to-shoulder, thrusting their short swords into the enemy.

mountains, Caesar rushed his men toward the Rhone River, where a crisis already awaited his arrival. More than 300,000 members of the Helvetii tribe were migrating west in search of fertile land on the Atlantic coast of Gaul. To get there, they needed to cross Roman territory, and Caesar did not trust that their intentions were peaceful.

When he reached the Rhone, Caesar put his engineers to work. They destroyed a bridge across the river and built a 16-foot-high earthen wall that stretched for 19 miles along the west bank. The Helvetii could only cross the river in small groups on makeshift rafts. As soon as each group reached the west bank, they were cut down by a barrage of javelins and arrows from the wall.

Stopped in their tracks by a single legion, the Helvetii turned north to try another route.

Caesar rushed to northern Italy and took command of five more legions. Marching north with a force that now totaled 30,000 men, he chased the Helvetii to Bibracte, in central Gaul.

Caesar stationed his legions on high ground and drew the Helvetii into battle. "Our men easily broke up the enemy's mass formation, and, having achieved this, drew their swords and charged," Caesar wrote later in his battlefield journal. "In the end, the wounds and toil of battle were too much for [the enemy] . . . and [they] retreated."

Three days after the battle, the Helvetii surrendered and agreed to resettle in their old homeland. By Caesar's reckoning, only 110,000 of them returned home. Over a quarter of a million Helvetii had been dispersed, sold into slavery, or killed in battle.

Caesar had won his first great victory in Gaul, and he made sure that all of Rome learned the details of the campaign.

During each of the eight years that Caesar spent in Gaul, he sent an annual report to the Senate. Most likely, he included glowing accounts from the journals he kept. The journals themselves, which became known as the *Commentaries on the Gallic and Civil Wars*, were

CAESAR DICTATES HIS ACCOUNT of yet another victory in
Gaul. The Gauls were fierce warriors, but they were no match
for Caesar's strategies.

probably read aloud in the Forum to rapt crowds eager
to hear about the exploits of their latest military hero.

When Caesar had left for Gaul, Romans wondered
whether he had what it took to be a great commander.
He was a silver-tongued politician with a gift for rousing
the masses—but was he ruthless and strong in battle?

Now there was no doubt.

CHAPTER 10

Conquering Gaul

LEAVING A TRAIL OF DESTRUCTION behind him, Caesar wins a reputation as a war hero.

AFTER HEARING ABOUT THE FATE OF the Helvetii tribe in the summer of 58 B.C., many of Gaul's tribal leaders came to Caesar and pledged their allegiance. Those who remained independent became targets for Caesar's mighty legions.

Over the next five years, Caesar swept north and west through Gaul. He seized supplies and drafted troops from local communities. Tribes that chose to resist fell one by one under Caesar's onslaught.

Caesar fought with decisiveness, ingenuity, and ruthlessness. In 56 B.C., he built a fleet of oar-powered galleys to send against the rebellious seafaring Veneti tribe of northwest Gaul. He had no luck ramming the thick-hulled Gallic ships, so he used long poles tipped with sharp hooks to cut the ropes of the Veneti sails.

During the same year, he marched on the Germanic tribes of the northeast. To cross the Rhine River into Germanic territory, his men built what was then the world's longest bridge—and they did it in just ten days.

Both the Germans and the Veneti suffered mightily for their resistance. In the German lands, Caesar had his men burn all the farmland they could find, leaving thousands homeless and desperate for food. He reserved the harshest punishment for the Veneti. He ordered several hundred of their leaders beheaded and had thousands of people sold into slavery.

While Caesar went to great lengths to instill fear

in his enemies, he inspired only loyalty in his men. He often led troops into battle himself. He sent his horse to the rear to ensure that he could not flee faster than his men. Caesar was strict and demanding but seemed to care deeply for his soldiers. He spoke with them as equals. He doubled their pay and made sure they had the best weapons and armor. According to the ancient historian Plutarch, soldiers with merely average skills "became

CAESAR'S LEGIONS IN BATTLE on the island of Britain.
News of the invasion thrilled Caesar's supporters in Rome,
who were growing more numerous by the day.

invincible and ready to confront any danger once it was a question of fighting for Caesar's honor and glory."

For his part, Caesar made sure that the glory he earned on the battlefield brought him power in Rome. In the spring of 56 B.C., he met with Crassus and Pompey in the northern Italian town of Luca to renew their alliance. Crassus and Pompey agreed to get themselves elected co-consuls and use their positions to extend Caesar's command in Gaul for another five years.

Pompey and Crassus returned to Rome with a band of thuggish soldiers who made their presence known on election day. The two men won their consulships amidst street battles brutal enough to leave Pompey spattered with another man's blood.

Assured of five more years in Gaul, Caesar gave his legions plenty to do. He campaigned once more against rebellious Germans. He led an invasion force across the English Channel to Britain. Though he was driven off by a force of tribesmen with horses and chariots, reports of the invasion thrilled the public back in Rome.

CAESAR BESIEGES the city of Bourges. This battle, like
so many others in Gaul, was a complete victory for the Romans.
The historian Plutarch claimed that Caesar killed one million enemy
warriors during his rampage through Gaul.

In 53 B.C., Caesar met his sternest test. A Gallic tribal leader named Vercingetorix convinced 40 tribes to join forces in rebellion against the Romans. Rather than confront the powerful legions head on, Vercingetorix shadowed them, launching small attacks and burning towns and fields to deny supplies to the Roman soldiers.

The rebels tormented Caesar for several months until he finally trapped them in the walled hilltop town of Alesia. In another display of engineering skill, Caesar built a 12-foot-high wall around the town and booby-trapped the ground with sharpened stakes and deep pits. Then he settled in to starve the Gauls into submission.

The siege lasted little more than a month. A relief force summoned by Vercingetorix tried to break Caesar's hold on the city, but the Romans fought them off. Vercingetorix was forced to surrender. The rebel leader put on his best armor, rode out to Caesar, dismounted, and sat at the victor's feet until he was led away.

CHAPTER 11

The Die Is Cast!

Forced into a painful choice, CAESAR PLUNGES ROME INTO CIVIL WAR.

BY 50 B.C., CAESAR HAD SUBDUED ALL OF Gaul from the Atlantic Ocean to the Rhine River. He had brought 200,000 square miles of western Europe under Roman control. In the process, he had amassed enough wealth in tribute and plunder to pay off his massive debts.

Caesar had made himself one of the richest men in Rome—and one of the most popular as well. The Senate had voted three times to hold public thanksgiving celebrations in his honor. A massive construction project was underway in the Forum to commemorate his victories.

With his work finished in Gaul, Caesar wanted to return to Rome to enjoy the fruits of his success. He was ready to march through the streets in triumph, to spend the riches he'd acquired, to rise again to the consulship. He was looking forward to assuming his place as the ruler of the Roman Republic.

But for all his popularity, Caesar still had plenty of enemies in Rome. Many of them wanted revenge for Caesar's strong-arm tactics during his year as consul, and they vowed to put him on trial if he returned.

In the past five years, Caesar had also lost valuable allies. Crassus had been killed in battle in 53 B.C. Caesar's daughter, Julia, who had been married to Pompey, died in childbirth. The death not only left both men deeply saddened but weakened the bond between them.

By the time Caesar's Gallic command neared its end, he and Pompey were no longer on speaking terms.

Pompey was arguably the most powerful man in Rome. He commanded several legions stationed in Spain and liked to boast that he had only to stomp his foot and armies would rise from the soil of Italy to follow him. In recent years, however, he had grown jealous of Caesar's fame and wealth. Pompey allied with the optimates and insisted that Caesar give up command of his troops before returning to Rome. Through envoys to the Senate, Caesar responded that he would give up his legions only if Pompey gave up his.

By the beginning of 49 B.C., the standoff between the two generals had brought the Republic to the brink of civil war. Angry debates rang out across the Forum from the Senate meeting hall. Many senators attempted to pass laws demanding that Caesar give up his command. Each time, Caesar's two closest allies, the tribunes Quintus Cassius and Mark Antony, vetoed the measures.

Finally, on January 7, the Senate ignored Cassius and Antony and issued a special decree placing Rome under martial law. Quintus Cassius and Marc Antony, fearing for their lives, disguised themselves and fled Rome. When word of the decree reached Caesar, he took it for what it was: a call for Pompey to use force to keep Caesar out.

Caesar had set up camp along a small river called the Rubicon, which marked the border between Gaul and Rome. He had just one legion and about 300 cavalry with him. But he felt the decree had forced him to make a decision: Should he cross the river with his troops? Doing so would plunge the Republic into a civil war and pit his lone legion against Pompey and all the official might of Rome.

In the end, Caesar felt he had no choice. If he returned to Rome without his army, his enemies would put him on trial for his abuse of power as consul. If he stayed in Gaul, he would be denied the fruits of his success. If he delayed, he would give Pompey time to raise new legions in Italy and bring his army back from Spain.

CAESAR DEFIED POMPEY AND THE SENATE by leading his army across the Rubicon River and marching toward Rome. This invasion doomed the Republic to suffer yet another bloody civil war.

Shortly after dawn on the morning of January 10, 49 B.C., Caesar joined his men on the Gallic side of the Rubicon. He set horses free as an offering to the gods. Then he cried out, "The die is cast," and led his loyal troops across the Rubicon and into the Roman heartland.

CHAPTER 12

Rome Divided

Caesar and Pompey BATTLE IT OUT ON THREE CONTINENTS.

Nₑws of Caesar's march on Rome shocked Pompey, who was not prepared to defend the city. The bulk of his fighting force was stationed 600 miles away in Spain, and no army had yet "risen from the soil" to defend him. The great war hero turned and fled, joined by most of the senators who had backed him.

Pompey raced south, gathering two legions, arms, and equipment as he marched. Caesar pursued him relentlessly down the eastern coast of Italy. Towns along the way opened their gates to welcome Caesar. His army swelled with local recruits and battle-hardened soldiers arriving from Gaul.

As he swept southward, Caesar sent envoys to Pompey requesting a meeting. "What I wanted most of all was the chance to have an interview with Pompey," he wrote.

But Caesar's old ally refused to meet with him. Instead, Pompey gathered as large an army as he could at the port city of Brundisium. Then he escaped to Greece to train and equip a force strong enough to take on the army that had conquered all of Gaul.

Caesar headed for Rome, hoping to put together a Senate from its remaining members and take control of the Republic. The great orator Cicero, however, was convinced that there was no Republic left to lead. Caesar, he believed, wanted to rule as a dictator, backed by the power of his army. "The sun seems to me to have disappeared from the universe," Cicero wrote in a letter to a friend.

In Rome, Caesar convened a poorly attended meeting of the Senate. He asked them to send an envoy to Greece to negotiate with Pompey. The senators voted to approve the motion, but no one volunteered to go.

With little hope of making peace, Caesar pursued the war with vigor. Lacking enough transport ships to take an invasion force to Greece, he decided to attack Pompey's soldiers in Spain. Before Caesar left, he broke into Rome's treasury and seized a fortune in gold and silver to fund the war.

Caesar swept through Spain in the summer of 49 B.C., and then returned for a showdown with Pompey in Greece. Refusing to wait for the warmer months, Caesar gathered seven legions—not all of them at full strength—and ferried them across the Adriatic Sea. Pompey had assembled and trained a force of 57,000 men, more than twice as large as Caesar's.

For eight months, Pompey tried to starve Caesar's army by blockading the coast. Finally, Caesar lured Pompey's troops to the Plain of Pharsalus and trapped

POMPEY FLEES after his defeat at the Battle of Pharsalus.
Pompey had begun the battle with twice as many
soldiers as Caesar. But Caesar's handpicked veterans were
able to encircle and destroy Pompey's army.

them against the River Enipeus. The final battle of the civil war was short and fierce. Caesar claimed to have killed 15,000 men, most of whom were Greek recruits.

Pompey himself escaped from Pharsalus. He boarded a ship and sailed for Egypt, with Caesar following close behind. The great Egyptian pharaohs had long been trading partners with Rome, and they had helped arm Pompey's army in Greece. Pompey had reason to believe he would be welcomed as an honored guest.

For the aging Roman general, it was the latest in a string of miscalculations. It would prove to be his last.

CHAPTER 13

Murder on the Nile

POMPEY MEETS A SHOCKING FATE, and Caesar is drawn into an Egyptian civil war.

CAESAR SAILED INTO ALEXANDRIA, EGYPT'S capital city, just three days behind Pompey. He was greeted with a gruesome surprise. Envoys from the young Egyptian pharaoh, Ptolemy XIII, presented him with a basket. In it lay Pompey's head.

Ptolemy's advisers—the pharaoh was in his early teens—knew before Pompey's arrival that the Roman general had lost the war. Sure that Caesar was soon to follow, they wanted to side with the victor. At the time, the advisers were locked in a struggle for the throne with Ptolemy's 21-year-old sister, Cleopatra. They needed Caesar's support and decided to kill Pompey in order to get it.

They couldn't have made a more disastrous mistake. Caesar wept when he saw the head of one of Rome's great heroes rotting in the Egyptian sun. He insisted that he had only wanted to make peace with his former ally and son-in-law. "What a gift to have sent!" he shouted at the envoys. "Tell your king that I count it more of an insult to me than to Pompey."

Caesar led 4,000 legionnaires into the heart of Alexandria and stormed the royal palace, taking Ptolemy hostage. He moved into luxurious quarters and refused to leave. Egyptian troops trapped Caesar and his legions in the palace compound. Caesar sent for reinforcements, and the two sides settled into a long stalemate.

One night, a servant arrived in Caesar's rooms with an unusual gift. He set a laundry bag on the floor and opened it to reveal a beautiful young woman. Cleopatra

CAESAR RECOILS at the gift of Pompey's head. Although the two men had fought a death match for control of Rome, Caesar had never lost respect for his longtime ally.

had smuggled herself in to see the Roman conqueror, and she begged Caesar to help her seize the throne from her brother. Cleopatra was witty, cunning, and intelligent, and Caesar fell in love with her. He pledged to make her queen of Egypt.

In January 47 B.C., Caesar's reinforcements arrived at the mouth of the Nile River. A large Egyptian force left Alexandria to confront them. Caesar let Ptolemy go and slipped out of Alexandria to join his new army. On the banks of the Nile, 20,000 Egyptian

CLEOPATRA presents herself to Caesar. The young queen was locked in a struggle with her brother Ptolemy for control of Egypt. Caesar fought to protect her claim to the throne.

CAESAR'S MEN CHARGE the Lighthouse of Alexandria
during the war against Ptolemy. During this battle, Caesar was
surrounded by enemy soldiers. He escaped by jumping into
the harbor and swimming to a Roman ship.

soldiers, armed with long pikes, faced off against
Caesar's troops. The Romans and their allies sent
a shower of javelins down on them. Then they
fought their way inside the range of the pikes and
destroyed the Egyptians in hand-to-hand combat.
Ptolemy tried to flee down the Nile, but fell
overboard when his ship was attacked. He was pulled

underwater by his heavy golden armor and was never seen again.

Caesar had added yet another land to his growing list of conquests.

By this time the great commander was tired. He was 52 years old. He had been at war for more than a decade, since he first took up his command in Gaul. He knew that he still had to resolve Rome's civil war. A group of Pompey's allies had raised an army and taken it to North Africa, where they were planning a new assault on Italy. But the prospect of a rest must have seemed irresistible.

Caesar boarded Cleopatra's royal barge and, with the young queen of Egypt as his companion, spent the next three months sailing on the Nile.

In the summer, Caesar finally prepared to return to Rome. He stationed three legions in Egypt to defend Roman interests and help Cleopatra stay in power. The gesture probably had some personal importance to Caesar: Cleopatra was said to be pregnant with his child.

VENI, VIDI, VICI

BEFORE RETURNING TO ROME FROM EGYPT, Caesar won a battle and summed it up with one of the most famous quotes of all time.

Pharnaces, ruler of a small kingdom near the Province of Asia, had taken advantage of the Roman civil war to launch an attack on Roman lands.

In August 47 B.C., Caesar gathered four legions and sailed up the Mediterranean coast to confront Pharnaces. Within a few weeks, Caesar had destroyed the king's army, forced Pharnaces into flight, and brought order to the entire region. In a letter, Caesar described the campaign in just three Latin words: *Veni, Vidi, Vici*—"I came, I saw, I conquered."

ROMAN SOLDIERS HAIL CAESAR, their champion.

CHAPTER 14

Hail the Conqueror!

The returning hero
FINALLY GETS HIS DUE.

CAESAR RETURNED TO ROME IN OCTOBER 47 B.C. There he found Mark Antony feebly trying to maintain control of the city—while hosting wild parties and carrying on affairs. Caesar stayed just long enough to impose order on the Republic. He had himself named consul and got many of his allies elected to the other top offices. Then he sailed for North Africa, where he vanquished Pompey's allies in a six-month campaign.

Caesar returned to Rome in the summer of 46 B.C. and staged the most impressive party the city had ever seen. For all his conquests, he had never received a *triumph*—an elaborate ceremonial parade reserved for the most impressive military victories. Beginning on September 21, Caesar held a ten-day celebration that included no fewer than four triumphs—for his victories in Gaul, Egypt, Asia, and North Africa.

Hordes of people packed into Rome to watch the long processions of soldiers, floats, dancers, and priests. Flowers carpeted the streets. Caesar wore purple and gold and rode in a splendid chariot pulled by white horses. A slave stood behind him, holding a laurel wreath of victory over his head and whispering "Remember, you are mortal," to the triumphant general.

Prisoners from each of the campaigns were put on display for the crowds. Caesar had kept the Gallic rebel Vercingetorix alive for just this occasion. During the triumph for Gaul, he paraded the vanquished war chief through the streets in chains.

That very night, Caesar had his foe strangled to death in his prison cell.

Cleopatra traveled to Rome for the Egyptian triumph and watched from a reviewing stand. She held in her arms a 15-month-old son, whom she had named Caesarion (little Caesar).

Free feasts followed each triumph, with as many as 22,000 tables piled with food. Between the parades, Caesar arranged spectacles that recalled his days as Rome's entertainment director. In one show, 400 lions were set loose in a stadium and then killed. For another, Caesar had engineers divert the Tiber River to create a small lake so sailors could re-enact famous sea battles.

The gaudy theatrics were enough to make people forget for a moment that the fate of Rome now rested in the hands of a single man. But one smaller-scale production provided a sober moment. In one of the plays staged during the celebrations, an actor uttered the line, "He whom many fear must therefore fear many."

TO CELEBRATE HIS VICTORIES on three continents, Caesar and his soldiers paraded through the streets of Rome. They showed off the spoils of war—the prisoners, treasures, and exotic animals they had seized during the campaigns.

As if on cue, the entire audience turned and glanced at Caesar. What, they must have wondered, did the future hold for the general who had just killed thousands of Romans and seized the Republic by force?

Never in the history of Rome had one man held so much power, and Caesar didn't seem willing to give it up. Instead, he began building monuments to his success. He ordered a new Forum constructed near the original one and named it after himself. In the largest building—a temple dedicated to the goddess Venus—he placed a statue of Cleopatra.

Caesar's critics spread rumors that he was planning to move to Egypt, take Cleopatra as his queen, and rule Rome as a king. The Republic had been destroyed during the civil war, they claimed, and Caesar was not going to rebuild it.

Caesar ignored the muttering. He began the work that he thought was necessary to restore order to Rome.

CHAPTER 15

Dictator for Life

With the Republic reduced to a
memory, Caesar REMAKES ROME
IN HIS OWN IMAGE.

IN THE AFTERMATH OF THE CIVIL WAR,
Caesar surveyed his city. Crime rates had risen to the
point where ordinary citizens were afraid to walk the
streets. Desperately poor people packed the slums,
and wealthier citizens had fled the city in droves.

Given the condition of the city, many senators felt
that Rome needed a ruler with the power to impose
order quickly. They named Caesar dictator and later
extended his powers for ten years.

With astonishing speed, Caesar began to transform the Republic. To help foster loyalty inside Rome's rapidly growing borders, Caesar granted citizenship to residents of many provinces. To bring order to the city of Rome, he increased the penalties for theft and murder.

He sought to provide opportunities for the poor. He launched massive building projects that created thousands of new jobs. He set up new colonies in three of Rome's provinces—Carthage (in North Africa), Corinth (in Greece) and Seville (in Spain). Veterans and poor Romans who wanted a chance at a new life received free land in these colonies and were transported there free of charge.

Caesar also took steps to consolidate his power. He gave important positions to many of Pompey's former supporters in the hope of winning their allegiance. One such man was Marcus Brutus, who was the son of one of Caesar's longtime mistresses. Brutus had fought with Pompey at Pharsalus, but Caesar had always been fond of him and granted him a praetorship.

Caesar also enlarged the Senate to make room for more of his supporters. In 45 B.C., he demanded that the senators name him dictator for life. Partly out of fear and partly out of devotion, they obeyed.

As dictator for life, Caesar had absolute power. He controlled the army and the treasury. He was free

VETERAN SOLDIERS THANK CAESAR for his gift of free lands in the colony of Carthage, in North Africa.

to hand-pick consuls, overturn Senate and Assembly rulings, and order executions. Democracy was fading like a dream. "The Republic is nothing," Caesar pronounced, "just a name without substance or form."

Drunk with power, Caesar acted more and more like a king. He presided over the Senate from a golden throne. He had coins minted with his image on them—the first time in Rome's history that a living person had been honored that way. He dressed in the purple togas worn by the ancient Roman kings and had an ivory statue of himself placed among statues of the gods in the Forum.

Still, Caesar denied that he wanted total power. During a festival in February 44 B.C., he had Mark Antony offer him a king's crown. Caesar then made a show of rejecting it. "Jupiter alone is king of the Romans," he said, referring to the most powerful Roman god.

At this point, however, Caesar's enemies had already hatched a secret plot to end his dictatorship, and no public gesture could convince them to turn back.

MARC ANTONY offers Caesar the crown of Rome. Caesar
declined, but his show of modesty fooled almost no one.

Beware the Ides of March

A plan is hatched, and Caesar,
for once, CANNOT ESCAPE.

IN THE SPRING OF 44 B.C., CAESAR PLANNED
to head east for yet another military campaign. This
time, his target was to be Parthia (in present-day
Iran), the site of one of Alexander the Great's famous
victories. He would be gone for years.

The news made a small group of men vow to carry
out a dangerous mission before Caesar left.

By the beginning of that year, several dozen

senators had begun to meet in secret around the city. Among the leaders of the conspiracy was Marcus Brutus, whom Caesar had known since Brutus was a child. The plotters called themselves "The Liberators," and their plan was to assassinate the most powerful man in the history of Rome.

Caesar rose early on March 15, a date known as the Ides of March. Slaves carried him to the Senate in a litter. He passed a fortune teller who earlier in the week had warned him that something terrible would happen on this particular day. He jokingly called out, "The Ides of March are come!" She answered, "Aye, Caesar, but not gone."

On the way into the Senate, Caesar was approached by a Greek teacher who worked for Brutus and had caught word of the plot. The teacher urgently passed a note to Caesar, who merely stuffed it into a pile of papers he was carrying.

When Caesar took his seat in the Senate, a man named Lucius Tillius Cimber approached him. He asked

AFTER DREAMING that her husband would be murdered,
Calpurnia begged Caesar to stay home on the Ides of March. Caesar
ignored her warning, as he ignored others who predicted his murder.

Caesar to grant a pardon to his brother, who had been
banned from Rome for siding with Pompey during the
civil war. As planned, about 20 senators crowded around
Caesar, pleading with him to grant the pardon.

Giving a prearranged signal, Cimber tugged on
Caesar's toga. Then the senators pulled out hidden
daggers and pressed in on Caesar. A man named Casca
struck the first blow. He was nervous and merely grazed
Caesar's shoulder. The great conqueror of Gaul and

Egypt tried to fight off Casca with the only weapon he had—his pen. The other plotters fell on Caesar with their daggers, slashing and stabbing.

For the first time in Caesar's life, there was no escape. When he saw Brutus in the group, Caesar stopped trying to fight. "You, too, my child?" he cried in despair. Then he pulled his toga over his face and collapsed.

CAESAR LIES DEAD ON THE FLOOR OF THE SENATE.
One of the assassins was Marcus Brutus, Caesar's longtime friend.
Brutus had remarked that killing Caesar was "necessary to
defend the liberty" of Rome.

The scene was grisly and chaotic. The plotters were splattered with blood, Caesar's and their own. Some had been accidentally injured by their own friends' daggers. When the senators finally dispersed, Caesar lay dead on the floor of the Senate, stabbed 23 times.

Brutus and the other assassins strode out of the Forum and walked calmly through the streets. One of them grabbed a hat normally worn by freed slaves and stuck it on a pole, symbolizing the liberty they thought they had recovered for Rome.

Back in the Senate, three of Caesar's slaves summoned the courage to approach their master's body. They gently placed Caesar onto a litter and carried him home to his house on the Forum.

Three days later, the Senate held a massive public funeral for their dictator. Despite the assassins' claim that they had liberated Rome, the common people didn't see it that way. When Caesar's will was read aloud at his funeral, it was revealed that he had left money for a lavish public garden and gift of cash to every citizen.

SLAVES CARRY CAESAR'S CORPSE from the Senate to his home.
Caesar had succeeded in his ambition to become master of Rome,
but his reign ended as violently as it had begun.

When the ceremony ended, rioters took over the city
streets, demanding vengeance for the murder of the
dictator who had used his power for the common good.

VIOLENCE BREAKS OUT during Caesar's funeral. Mobs of Romans who had supported Caesar roamed the streets, murdering people they thought were responsible for the assassination.

Wicked?

Caesar's assassins, the self-proclaimed "Liberators," claimed they wanted to restore democracy to Rome. If that really was their aim, they failed miserably.

Caesar left most of his vast estate to Octavian, an 18-year-old grand nephew. After 15 years of political turmoil and civil war, Octavian took sole control of Rome. Gone were the days of open debates and popular elections. For the next four centuries, control of Rome's vast empire would pass from strongman to strongman, usually through family lines.

Was Caesar responsible for the downfall of one of history's first experiments in democracy? There is no question that he seized power and showed no signs of giving it up. But the Republic was already falling apart. Desperately poor people crowded the slums of Rome. Wealthy aristocrats bought their way into office. Military commanders acquired vast amounts of power and wealth and used it to impose their will on the people.

Caesar, at least, often used his power for the people's benefit. He created jobs and distributed land to the poor. He gave his rivals a place in government rather than throwing them in jail or executing them as so many other tyrants have done. He was convinced that he was saving Rome, not destroying it.

As a commander, Caesar was ruthless to his enemies. One million people may have died during his military campaigns. Another million were probably sold into slavery. At the same time, he inspired tremendous loyalty in his own soldiers. He rewarded their bravery with gratitude, cash, and land.

Did Caesar honestly care about the welfare of Rome's common people? Or did he just use the people to gain power for himself? Was he devoted to the glory of Rome, or merely to the glory of Caesar?

In the end, it may not matter what his intentions were. The path he chose did not lead back to democracy.

And the men who followed Caesar were not as willing to wield their power for the good of the people.

More than 2,000 years since his death, Caesar is still one of the most talked-about figures in history. And we remember him not so much for his policies as for his relentless drive for power. The word for "emperor" in German is *kaiser*, in Russian it is *tsar*. Both words trace their origin back to Caesar, who was for a fleeting moment the most powerful man on earth.

READINGS FROM ANCIENT TIMES

When studying people and events of the past, historians seek firsthand evidence. They turn to primary sources, original documents or objects created during the time they are studying. The first of these readings, from the journals of Julius Caesar, is an example of a primary source.

Few primary sources survive from ancient times. So historians also rely on secondary sources, created after actual events took place. Especially helpful are accounts by ancient historians, which often draw from original materials that are now lost.

Two such historians are the Greek writer Plutarch and the Roman writer Suetonius. In the following readings, Plutarch describes Caesar's assassination, and Suetonius explains why some people thought the killing was just.

All sources, whether primary or secondary, must be examined for reliability and possible bias. Historians understand that such accounts provide different points of view about the same events. Taken together, they bring us to a fuller understanding of the past.

FROM THE GALLIC WAR

Julius Caesar kept a journal during his time in Gaul (58-50 B.C.). In this excerpt, he evokes the chaos of the Battle of the Sabis (57 B.C), in which his troops overcame the Nervians, who lived in the north of France and modern Belgium. Caesar portrays himself as brave in battle and supporting his troops. He refers to himself in the third person, making the account seem more objective.

After haranguing the Tenth Legion Caesar started for the right wing. There Caesar beheld his troops hard driven, and the men of the Twelfth Legion, with their standards collected in one place, so closely packed that they hampered each other for fighting. All the centurions of the fourth cohort had been slain, and the standard-bearer likewise, and the standard was lost; almost all the centurions of the other cohorts were either wounded or killed.... The rest of the men were tiring, and some of the rearmost ranks, abandoning the fight, were retiring to avoid the missiles; the enemy were not ceasing to move upwards in front from the lower ground, and were pressing hard on either flank. The condition of affairs, as he saw, was critical indeed, and there was no support that could be sent up. Taking therefore a shield from a soldier of the rearmost ranks, as he himself was come thither without a shield, he went forward into the first line, and, calling on the centurions by name, and cheering on the rank and file, he bade them advance and extend the companies, that they might ply swords more easily. His coming brought hope to the troops and renewed their spirit; each man of his own accord, in sight of the commander-in-chief, desperate as his own case might be, was fain to do his utmost....

Perceiving that the Seventh Legion, which had formed up near at hand, was also harassed by the enemy, Caesar instructed the tribunes to close the legions gradually together, and then, wheeling, to advance against the enemy. This was done; and as one soldier supported another, and they did not fear that their rear would be surrounded by the enemy, they began to resist more boldly and to fight more bravely... and Titus Labienus, having taken possession of the enemy's camp, and observed from the higher ground what was going forward in our own camp, sent the Tenth Legion to support our troops.

Their arrival wrought a great change in the situation. Even such of our troops as had fallen under stress of wounds propped themselves against their shields and renewed the fight; then the sutlers [merchants], seeing the panic of the enemy, met their armed assault even without arms; finally, the cavalry, to obliterate by valor the disgrace of their flight, fought at every point in the effort to surpass the legionaries. The enemy, however, even when their hope of safety was at an end, displayed a prodigious courage. When their front ranks had fallen, the next stood on the prostrate forms and fought from them; when these were cast down, and the corpses were piled up in heaps, the survivors, standing as it were upon a mound, hurled darts on our troops, or caught and returned our pikes. Not without reason, therefore, was it to be concluded that these were men of a great courage, who had dared to cross a very broad river, to climb very high banks, and to press up over most unfavorable ground. These were tasks of the utmost difficulty, but greatness of courage had made them easy.

Source: Julius Caesar, *The Gallic War,* trans. by H. J. Edwards, Loeb Classical Library (Cambridge: Harvard University Press, 1917).

From The Lives of Noble Grecians and Romans

Writing about A.D. 75, Greek historian Plutarch describes Julius Caesar's assassination in the Senate on the Ides of March (March 15, 44 B.C.). Marcus Brutus, whom Caesar considered a friend, led a group of senators in the attack.

Now when the senate was gone in before to the chamber where they were to sit, the rest of the company placed themselves close about Caesar's chair, as if they had some suit to make to him.... Trebonius, in the meanwhile, engaged Antony's attention at the door, and kept him in talk outside. When Caesar entered, the whole senate rose up to him. As soon as he was sat down, the men all crowded round about him, and set Tillius Cimber, one of their own number, to intercede in behalf of his brother that was banished; they all joined their prayers with his, and took Caesar by the hand, and kissed his head and his breast. But he putting aside at first their supplications, and afterwards, when he saw they would not desist, violently rising up, Tillius with both hands caught hold of Caesar's robe and pulled it off from his shoulders, and Casca, that stood behind him, drawing his dagger, gave him the first, but a slight wound, about the shoulder. Caesar snatching hold of the handle of the dagger, and crying out aloud in Latin, "Villain Casca, what do you?" he, calling in Greek to his brother, bade him come and help. And by this time, finding himself struck by a great many hands, and looking around about him to see if he could force his way out, when he saw Brutus with his dagger drawn against him, he let go Casca's hand, that he had hold of and covering his head with his robe, gave up his body to their blows. And they so eagerly pressed towards the body, and so many daggers were hacking together, that they cut one another; Brutus, particularly, received a wound in his hand, and all of them were besmeared with the blood.

Source: Plutarch, *The Lives of Noble Grecians and Romans,* trans. by John Dryden and ed. by Arthur Hugh Clough, vol. 3 (Boston: Little, Brown and Co., 1902).

FROM THE LIVES OF THE CAESARS

In this excerpt from a work written about A.D. 121, Roman historian Suetonius explains why some believed that Caesar was "justly slain." Other historians described Caesar's love of luxury and power, but Suetonius also notes his slights against the Senate and disregard of Roman law.

Yet after all, his other actions and words so turn the scale, that it is thought that Caesar abused his power and was justly slain. For not only did he accept excessive honors, such as an uninterrupted consulship, the dictatorship for life, and the censorship of public morals, as well as the forename Imperator, the surname of Father of his Country, a statue among those of the kings, and a raised couch in the orchestra; but he also allowed honors to be bestowed on him which were too great for mortal man: a golden throne in the House and on the judgment seat; a chariot and litter in the procession at the circus; temples, altars, and statues beside those of the gods; a special priest, an additional college of the Luperci, and the calling of one of the months by his name. In fact, there were no honors which he did not receive or confer at pleasure.

He held his third and fourth consulships in name only, content with the power of the dictatorship conferred on him at the same time as the consulships. Moreover, in both years he substituted two consuls for himself for the last three months.... When one of the consuls suddenly died the day before the Kalends of January, he gave the vacant office for a few hours to a man who asked for it. With the same disregard of law and precedent he named magistrates for several years to come... and admitted to the House men who had been given citizenship, and in some cases half-civilized Gauls. He assigned the charge of the mint and of the public revenues to his own slaves, and gave the oversight and command of the three legions which he had left at Alexandria to a favorite of his called Rufio, son of one of his freedmen.

Source: Suetonius, *The Lives of the Caesars,* vol. 1, trans. by J. C. Rolfe, Loeb Classical Library (Cambridge: Harvard University Press, 1914).

PROJECT IDEAS

Now you have read a modern biography of Julius
Caesar, as well as writings by and about him from
ancient times. Use the evidence you have gathered
to complete one or more of these projects.

Interview with Julius Caesar

Imagine that you have an opportunity to interview Julius
Caesar. Prepare an interview, writing both questions and
answers. Base your interview on historical facts. Decide
on the tone: Will it be neutral, friendly, or challenging?

Speaking from Caesar's Point of View

Prepare and present a speech from the point of view
of Julius Caesar defending himself against wicked
allegations. Provide careful reasoning for your argument,
and stick to the facts. Include the following points:

- Your positive and negative impact on Rome and its
  citizens
- Your will
- Your lifestyle

Interpret an Ancient Reading

In *The Lives of the Caesars*, Suetonius explains why some people thought Caesar's assassination was justified. Write a paragraph explaining this justification.

Wicked Tweets

Create two or three tweets from Caesar about important events in his life. Events might include his victories in Gaul, his confrontation with the pirates, and his crossing of the Rubicon. Be sure to limit your tweets to 140 characters and include hashtags.

Here's an example of a tweet from Caesar's assassins:

Dictator for life? Not on our watch! Hey, JC, you should have listened to that fortune teller. @LiberatorsWithDaggers #IdesofMarch

Mark Antony

(c. 83–30 B.C.)

Mark Antony was a Roman general and politician. He served bravely under Caesar during the conquest of Gaul (most of today's France). He also supported Caesar during the civil war (49–48 B.C.) with Pompey. When Caesar was killed in 44 B.C., Antony seized power for himself.

Marcus Brutus

(c. 85–42 B.C.)

Marcus Brutus was a Roman politician. He sided with Pompey and against Julius Caesar in the civil war (49–48 B.C.). Caesar pardoned Brutus after Pompey's defeat. But Brutus joined the plot to assassinate Caesar in 44 B.C. Defeated in battle in 42 B.C, Brutus killed himself.

Cato

(95–46 B.C.)

Cato was a leading Roman politician. When civil war erupted in 49 B.C., Cato supported Pompey. Upon Pompey's defeat at Pharsalus in 48 B.C., he fled to Africa and governed Utica until Caesar's victory at Thapsus. Fearing the prospect of a dictatorship by Caesar, Cato killed himself in 46 B.C.

Cicero
(106–43 B.C.)

Cicero was a politician and ancient Rome's greatest orator. He disapproved of Julius Caesar becoming dictator for life, believing Caesar would destroy the Roman Republic. Cicero took no part in Caesar's assassination in 44 B.C., but he approved of it. Caesar's successors ordered Cicero's murder in 43 B.C.

Cinna
(c. 130–84 B.C.)

Cinna was a Roman politician. He became consul in 87 B.C. but was soon expelled for his views. Cinna allied himself with another politician, Marius. By the end of 87 B.C. the two men controlled Rome. When Marius died in 86 B.C., Cinna ruled alone until 84 B.C., when he was murdered by his own troops.

Cleopatra
(69–30 B.C.)

Cleopatra was one of Egypt's most famous queens. She ruled with her brother Ptolemy XIII from 51 B.C. until 49 B.C., when he exiled her. With the help of Julius Caesar, Cleopatra resumed her rule in 47 B.C., first with her brother Ptolemy XIV and then with Ptolemy XV, her son. After her death, Egypt fell under Roman rule.

Crassus
(c. 115–53 B.C.)

Crassus was a Roman politician and general. He was also one of the richest men in ancient Rome, along with Pompey and Julius Caesar. In 60 B.C., Crassus, Caesar, and Pompey joined in a political alliance called the First Triumvirate. Crassus died in battle in the war on Parthia (in present-day Iran) in 53 B.C.

Marius
(c. 157–86 B.C.)

Marius was a Roman general, politician, and Julius Caesar's uncle. He served as consul in 107 B.C. and from 104 through 100 B.C. In 88 B.C., Sulla, his old rival, marched his troops into Rome, forcing Marius out. In 87 B.C., Marius's army recaptured Rome. He became consul again in 86 B.C.

Pompey
(106–48 B.C.)

Pompey was a Roman politician and military leader. He served Rome during a revolt by its allies in Italy (91–88 B.C.) and in many other campaigns. His military exploits earned him great power and wealth. But he was defeated by Julius Caesar during the civil war (49–48 B.C.) and assassinated in Egypt in 48 B.C.

Spartacus
(?–71 B.C.)

Spartacus, a shepherd from Thrace, was trained as a gladiator by the Romans. In 73 B.C. he escaped and raised an army of some 70,000 runaway slaves. His forces devastated Roman armies but were defeated by them at the Silarus River, where Spartacus was killed.

Sulla
(c. 138–78 B.C.)

Sulla was a Roman general and politician. He proved himself in battle during a revolt by Rome's allies (91–88 B.C.). He used those skills again in 82 B.C., when he led his armies into Rome and forced the Senate to name him dictator. After resigning as dictator and serving as consul in 80 B.C., Sulla retired.

Vercingetorix
(?–46 B.C.)

Vercingetorix was a chieftain of the Arverni tribe of Gaul. He resisted Julius Caesar's conquest of Gaul in 52 B.C., leading the Arverni and other Gauls in revolt. After initial successes, his forces were defeated by Caesar. He was paraded through the streets of Rome as part of Caesar's Gallic triumph and then executed.

Timeline of Terror

100: Julius Caesar is born in Rome.

73–71: Spartacus leads 70,000 slaves in a rebellion; Caesar may be involved in quashing it.

c. 85: Caesar's father dies.

80–78: Caesar serves in the Province of Asia and is awarded the Civic Crown.

c. 69: Caesar delivers a speech honoring his aunt Julia and h[er] family. He is elected quaesto[r] and serves in Spain.

100

81: Caesar refuses Sulla's order to divorce his wife.

c. 72: Caesar is elected military tribune, his first elected office.

88: Sulla marches on Rome after his command is taken from him.

75: Caesar is captured by pirates on the way to Rhodes, and ends up crucifying them.

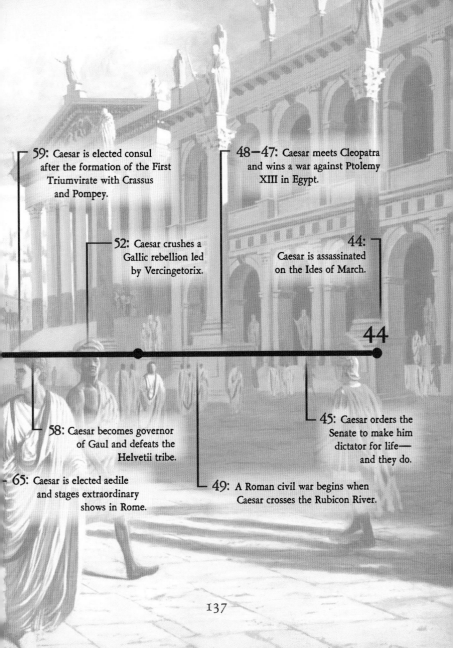

59: Caesar is elected consul after the formation of the First Triumvirate with Crassus and Pompey.

48–47: Caesar meets Cleopatra and wins a war against Ptolemy XIII in Egypt.

52: Caesar crushes a Gallic rebellion led by Vercingetorix.

44: Caesar is assassinated on the Ides of March.

44

58: Caesar becomes governor of Gaul and defeats the Helvetii tribe.

45: Caesar orders the Senate to make him dictator for life— and they do.

65: Caesar is elected aedile and stages extraordinary shows in Rome.

49: A Roman civil war begins when Caesar crosses the Rubicon River.

GLOSSARY

aedile (EE-dile) *noun* official of the Roman Republic who was responsible for maintaining public buildings and streets and managing public festivals

censor (SEN-sur) *noun* official of the Roman Republic who served as census taker and supervised public conduct and morals

chariot (CHA-ree-uht) *noun* in ancient Rome, a vehicle pulled by a team of horses; chariots raced in stadiums called circuses

citizen (SIT-i-sin) *noun* in the Roman Republic, a male who had the right to vote and was exempt from paying taxes

consul (KON-suhl) *noun* official elected by the Roman Senate to head the Roman government and command the army in times of war; two consuls served at a time, and could cancel each other's decisions

crucify (KROO-suh-fye) *verb* to put someone to death by nailing them to a cross

democratic (dem-oh-KRAT-ik) *adjective* describing a system of government in which the people choose their leaders in free elections

dictator (DIK-tay-tur) *noun* in the Roman Republic, an official who ruled with unlimited power for a six-month term

Forum (FOR-um) *noun* the open public square where Romans came to worship, trade, and conduct government business

galley (GAL-ee) *noun* a long boat with oars, used in ancient times

gladiator (GLAD-ee-ay-tur) *noun* a warrior who fought against other gladiators or fierce animals to entertain the ancient Romans

javelin (JAV-uh-luhn) *noun* a light throwing spear

legion (LEE-juhn) *noun* in the late Roman Republic, a military unit of 5,000 armored soldiers, each armed with a short sword and two javelins

legislation (lej-uh-SLAY-shuhn) *noun* laws that have been proposed or made

lictor (LICK-tur) *noun* a bodyguard of a magistrate in ancient Rome *magistrates* (MAJ-uh-strates) *noun* the top government officials of the Roman Republic, including censors, consuls, praetors, quaestors, and aediles

optimate (OP-tuh-mit) *noun* a member of a political group representing the interests of the noble families of the Roman Republic

oratory (OR-uh-tor-ee) *noun* the art of formal speaking in public

patrician (puh-TRISH-un) *noun* a member of a noble family in ancient Rome

Popular Assembly (POP-yuh-lur uh-SEM-blee) *noun* in the Roman Republic, a legislative body made up of Roman citizens who were not senators

populare (pawp-oo-LAR-ay) *noun* a member of a political group representing the interests of the poor citizens of the Roman Republic

praetor (PREE-tur) *noun* the second-highest political office of the Roman Republic; duties included administering justice and commanding an army in the absence of a consul

prosecute (PROSS-uh-kyoot) *verb* to carry out legal action in a court of law against a person accused of a crime

province (PROV-uhnss) *noun* in the Roman Republic, a conquered foreign territory that was ruled by a governor

quaestor (KWESS-tur) *noun* an official who managed the finances of Rome or one of its provinces

republic (ri-PUB-lik) *noun* a form of government in which citizens elect representatives to manage the government

Senate (SEN-it) *noun* the Roman Republic's top lawmaking body; the Senate was made up of about 300 of Rome's richest and most powerful men

talent (TAL-uhnt) *noun* in ancient Rome, a large unit of weight or money, particularly a certain weight in gold or silver

tribune (TRIB-yoon) *noun* an official of the Roman Republic who was elected by the common citizens to represent them and protect their rights

trident (TRY-dint) *noun* a three-pronged spear

triumvirate (trye-UM-ver-rit) *noun* a group of three people sharing power

FIND OUT MORE

Here are some books with more information about Julius Caesar and his times.

NONFICTION

Beller, Susan Provost. *Roman Legions on the March: Soldiering in the Ancient Roman Army.* Minneapolis, MN: Twenty-First Century Books, 2008. (112 pages) *Describes what life was like for Roman soldiers, including their training, uniforms, weapons, and tactics.*

Galford, Ellen. *Julius Caesar: The Boy Who Conquered an Empire.* Washington, D.C.: National Geographic Children's Books, 2007. (64 pages) *This visually appealing book explores the life and times of Julius Caesar.*

Guerber, Helene. *The Story of the Romans.* N. Charleston, SC: CreateSpace Independent Publishing, 2014. (200 pages) *Brings history facts to life in storybook fashion.*

Haaren, John H., and A. B. Poland. *Famous Men of Ancient Rome: Lives of Julius Caesar, Nero, Marcus Aurelius and Others* (Dover Children's Classics). Mineola, NY: Dover Publications, 2005. (160 pages) *A memorable introduction to the famous leaders and great men of ancient Rome.*

Hunter, Nick. *Julius Caesar* (Hero Journals). Chicago, IL: Raintree, 2013. (48 pages) *Major events of Caesar's life, written as conversational, first-person journal entries.*

Lassieur, Allison. *The Ancient Romans (People of the Ancient World).* New York: Franklin Watts, 2004. (112 pages) *A lively and well-illustrated introduction to life in ancient Rome.*

Medina, Nico, and Tim Foley. *Who Was Julius Caesar?* New York: Grosset & Dunlap, 2014. (112 pages)
A highly readable account of Caesar's life.

Mellor, Ronald, and Marni McGee. *The Ancient Roman World* (The World in Ancient Times). New York: Oxford University Press, 2004. (190 pages)
This engaging book explores the history, culture, and leaders of ancient Rome.

Nardo, Don. *Julius Caesar: Roman General and Statesman* (Signature Lives). Minneapolis, MN: Compass Point Books, 2008. (112 pages)
A comprehensive look at the life of Julius Caesar.

Nardo, Don. *The Roman Republic* (World History). Detroit: Lucent Books, 2005. (112 pages)
A clearly written account of the rise and fall of the Roman Republic.

Saunders, Nicholas. *The Life of Julius Caesar.* Appleton, WI: School Specialty Publishing, 2006. (48 pages)
A factual look at Julius Caesar's rise to power in ancient Rome.

FICTION

Whitehead, Dan (adapter), and William Shakespeare. *Julius Caesar: The Graphic Novel* (Campfire Classics). Laurel, MD: Campfire Publishing, 2013. (112 pages)
William Shakespeare's classic retelling of actual historical events presented as a thrilling graphic adventure.

෴෴෴෴෴෴෴෴෴෴෴෴෴෴෴෴

Visit this Scholastic Web site for more information on Julius Caesar:

www.factsfornow.scholastic.com

Enter the keywords **Julius Caesar**

෴෴෴෴෴෴෴෴෴෴෴෴෴෴෴෴

INDEX

AUTHOR'S NOTE AND BIBLIOGRAPHY

Caesar wrote beautifully and corresponded with the important people of his time. After he died, an entire book was published that contained nothing but letters between him and Cicero. Letters between Caesar and Pompey filled another book. Many of Caesar's speeches and other writings were also published.

The problem for historians is that none of those volumes survived past ancient times. All that remains of Caesar's writings are his *Commentaries on the Gallic and Civil Wars* and a few letters to Cicero. Beyond that, much of what we know about Caesar comes from letters that Cicero wrote to his family and friends, and the work of four ancient writers, none of whom were alive at the same time as Caesar.

If I could unearth some of Caesar's lost writings, I'd look for answers to personal questions: What was Caesar like as a child? How did he really feel about Cleopatra? We know a lot about Caesar the military hero and Caesar the dictator. Caesar the human being is not as easy to discover.

The following works have proved most helpful in researching this book:

Freeman, Philip. *Julius Caesar*. New York: Simon & Schuster, 2008.

Goldsworthy, Adrian. *Caesar: Life of a Colossus*. New York and London: Yale University Press, 2006.

Matyszak, Philip. *Chronicle of the Roman Republic: The Rulers of Ancient Rome from Romulus to Augustus*. London: Thames & Hudson, Ltd., 2003.

Shelton, Jo-Ann. *As the Romans Did: A Sourcebook in Roman Social History, 2nd ed.* New York: Oxford University Press, 1998.

—Denise Rinaldo